Journey in the Mind's Eye of a Poet: A Search for Faith

BOOK FIVE (2010 TO 2011)

The Source

Tony Prewit

Journey in the Mind's Eye of a Poet: A Search for Faith
Book Five (2009 to 2010): The Source

copyright Tony Prewit, 2012

Published by Ridgeline Press
Silver City, New Mexico, U.S.A.
ISBN 978-0-9854487-4-5

Editing, book design, cover design, and production services by
Heidi Connolly, Harvard Girl Word Services
Cover artwork by Tony Prewit

Acknowledgments

I would like to thank my wife, Patricia Prewit, for the years of assistance in sorting, editing, and proofreading all my work. I thank her most of all for her being her and allowing me to continue to be the person she married. I would also like to thank Sarah Johnson, a professional proofreader, who offered intelligent suggestions in shaping these books and gave me a valuable critique of its quality and content. Finally, I would like to thank the friends who read the complete series, contributed valuable suggestions, and urged me to arrange it into the form it has become: Gretchen Van Auken, Charlie Mckee, and Gail Rein. I thank Raymond Hornbaker for the years of commitment to our late-night discussions. I would also like to mention the editor who helped with the final sculpture of these books, Heidi Connolly, whose vision, talent, and professional guidance have been invaluable.

Table of Contents

Prologue

These six books are written in a poetry/prose form, a process that spans thirty-five years and encompasses the gradual evolution into my inner search for a personal faith and belief in God. It is a poet's journal and also like a novel in poetry form, one in which I am the narrator as well as a main character. The poems document my gradual disengagement with traditional, conservative, evangelical Christianity as I built a belief and faith of my own. Although I certainly did not have this defined purpose when I started this journal, it matured this way over time to become collection of six books that record a journey in search of a faith I could call my own.

As I walk away from the Christianity in which I once believed without doubting the existence of a God, I continue to discover a place within where I am learning how to build my own faith. This writing is for those who are at a dead end or a crossroad in their belief, or in a dysfunctional relationship (so to speak) with their spiritual beliefs. One of my messages, therefore, is that our spiritual beliefs do not have to be unchangeable.

Consequently, these poems are not so much a criticism of Christianity as they are a process of learning to ask the right questions. Over time I have learned to be wary of those who do not want to hear my questions and who are defensive toward honest doubt and inquiry. Because I was trapped in a doctrine that did not allow me to express my belief in my own way, and because I wanted to keep my Christian friends, I kept silent for many years.

The poems in this work capture my observations and reflections about how I see life through the veil of my own struggle, and will hopefully allow others to consider the shortcomings of their own beliefs, or of any belief that does not allow for true dialog. Because none of us really knows the truth for sure when it comes to belief, it would appear that there are shortcomings in all spiritual belief systems, regardless of form. For that reason, we are left to ourselves to construct a satisfactory — and satisfying — faith.

The stunning effect of this pursuit is my finding that God gets larger from the inside out. This is where my journey has found its pleasure and its peace, even while admitting the sorrow and fear of the search.

I have wrestled with my soul along this path and it wrestled back, for what I was struggling with was my spiritual identity. In wrestling, I learned the value of putting forth the right questions rather than assuming I had the right answers.

In fact, questions have become answers in their own right for me, for a light turned on in the asking that helped illuminate my way. I further learned that without questions we have no way to really appreciate where we are going and why. As such, I am thankful that I realized the importance of questions within the arena of spiritual beliefs.

The six books in this series are (in order): *Journal of Time, Portals and Passages, The Book of the Lost and Found* or *Chasing Rainbows, Moods of War, The Source,* and *Another Day.*

Book One is the beginning of my realizations and observations of life, which I describe as "me looking inside me from the perspective of the outside me," and then, "me looking outside me from the perspective of the inside me." It is the discovery of my need for a faith in God of my own. Book Two is a confession of my dreams and the effect dreams can have upon one's life. Book Two also reveals my earliest thoughts concerning my spiritual beliefs, kept very secret until then, and how these secrets became a burden to my search for faith. In Books Three and Four I begin to focus my writing toward a more intense spiritual inquiry based on my discontentment with religious answers. These two works became like a great mountain I needed to climb, blocking the path of what I considered my "true" journey. One might also describe them as an inner wrestling match where the rule was to fight to the finish. In total these books are the recording of how I lost my past faith and discovered what I call "conflicts of faith." Hence, Book Five is the result of feeling as if I had reached the top of the mountain, had a good view of a long way down the road, and could tell that although the journey was long from over, I was sensing a peace that came from finding my own faith. Book Six is about learning to live with the faith I had created.

Phrases and Words

The phrase "Treat others as we want them to treat us" is the most frequently used phrase in these books, and it has become more important to me as the years have passed. It has become a part of the foundation of my own faith because no matter how I might try, it stuck with me, withstanding all inquiry, doubt, and question.

To treat others as we want them to treat us simply means to me that we value others as equal to ourselves and value their needs as important as our own. And that if we do not wish to be cheated, lied to, deceived, oppressed, or manipulated, then we should be willing not to cheat, lie, deceive, oppress, or manipulate others.

I use other Judeo-Christian terms such as "heaven" and "hell" and the duality of "good" and "evil." These terms and their meanings come from my own culture and western traditional Christian teaching. I do not necessarily consider these terms to be universally accepted as truth; they serve only as my own points of reference into my inner spiritual search.

My use of the word "God" in the masculine form is habit and based somewhat on the limitations of the English language. In my mind, God is of no gender, no religion, no race, no culture.

In some parts you may find the writing in these books somewhat redundant. The repetitiveness serves as an accurate picture of my perspective, however, for I believe we are all in the process of being formed and we repeat our thoughts and feelings until they either become a part of us or fade.

My style of writing is varied. It weaves poetry, commentary, and prose. I do not attempt to stay inside the lines of strict grammatical compliance. I give myself poetic license. I am much more concerned with content and the work's original form than with adherence to rules. You'll see I have also invented a few words along the way.

Initially, my poetry/journal was not produced as a neat stack of notebooks; instead, scattered notebooks, legal pads, single sheets, and scratch paper filled with writings piled up until the notebooks piled up on top of each other. They were in no real order. No, I did not have a neat stack at all. In fact, after thirty-five years' worth of notebooks had turned into a kind of organizational nightmare, I felt it was almost futile to even attempt to sort through it all. Common sense prevailed, however, and this six-book format is the result of sorting and compiling a presentable record of my writings.

As the Rain Strikes

as the rain strikes the window
with unexpected and unpredictable force

do these thoughts come
of my own design or choice?

they are an entity of their own
they travel in a realm of space only they know
till they rest upon my soul

from there they interrupt my own thoughts
and interject their own

> *there is no reasonable explanation*
> *why i would have these thoughts*
>
> *it is beyond me why i see*
> *what others do not nor care to.*

No Word Spoken or Written

1.
at the end of the day
there is no word spoken or written
that convinces me of the existence of God

i have searched within myself for the reality of God
and what i believe or do not believe has come from within
more than the word of the mouth or on the page.

2.
i believe no image of any person object or animal
represents God including Jesus.

3.
the God i perceive cannot be taught
rather we can only point where to search

to be taught of a God is to be taught how to imagine a God
but within is where we can find the true unseen God

it is the place where our faith meets our spirit
and it is there where we learn of this God

the point of it all is to become
a better human being while on the earth.

4.
if i ever come to a place within me
where i do not believe in God
it will also come from me
not from any spoken or written word

i absolve you and relieve you of the burden
of causing me to believe or not to believe in God

i hope that absolution makes you feel better
— it does me.

Many Paths, Same "Truths"

i believe there are many paths
that lead to the "truths" that God has for us

i believe God has made truth that way
that He has made paths that way
and that He has made us that way

looking within creates the entrance to these paths
and we must choose the path that suits us

there are many paths leading to the same truths.

Balance of Life

i enjoy a mountain scene from a vantage point on high
to see a long way off (what i call a view)
it is one way to balance my life

i have my best worship and prayer moments alone
at a great height

the same goes for my exercise routine
— another way to balance my life

i like driving through these mountains with my wife
i like watching a movie with my wife best
— yet another way to balance my life

> *the balance of life is my preference*
> *it is what i say it is*
> *what it is for me*
>
> *where does the spirit go after this life?*
> *no one knows*
>
> *so as to my time here with my spirit*
> *i will make the best of it*
> *that i can.*

The Source

the source is here for us all inside

go there and you will find it

you will know it

because it will accept you

without judgment.

Memory

it was probably 4:30 a.m.
when i used to rise from my bed to get dressed
and go quietly out the back door
down the steps to the backyard

and to the swing set
where i began to swing
as the sun gradually appeared
over the horizon

i remember once my mom appeared suddenly
in her nightgown
anxious and concerned
to ask me what i was doing

"swinging" i said
"i come out often"
she shook her head
"not anymore" she said
"not until i am up"

i tried once or twice
but it was too hard
to stand outside my parents' bedroom and wait

so i went out to swing as i had before
always before the sun was up
as if it had to be that way

in the hours alone i spoke
to the entity in my mind
as i suppose many children do

though these conversations
have not receded with childhood
and have continued till this day

this entity and i converse on many subjects
as i go along my journey
although now the conversation
is mostly in my dreams

my mother never asked again
why i liked to swing
before the sun rose

i never asked "why not?"

Day Vision
Mt. Lemmon, near Tucson, Arizona

the forest was thick
full quiet light shadows
everywhere reflecting dew
after a short rain
altitude about 7,500 feet

my friends and i made our way
on a narrow road
winding through the forest
limbs scraping against the sides
of the vw beetle

all was quiet till i said "stop"
and quickly squeezed out of the back seat
to run through the forest
to feel the pine needles cushioning my feet

i was eighteen years old

i ran about five minutes
as if guided though i knew not where
until i came upon my destination
an outdoor amphitheater
with seating for about 300

stunned i came upon it
no one else was around
and this is where my day-vision happened
at 2:00 p.m. march 1973

i do not know why
i had suddenly had to escape the vehicle
and run to this place and see this vision of myself
in this amphitheater with others
—all men in catholic monk-like robes—
where i was the youngest about nine years old

a very old man at the podium gave us instructions
preparing us for our journey to earth
as he spoke i looked up at all these men
wondering why they were all older than i

i looked out at a view as if on a ridge
and could see earth
and as the elderly man continued to talk
the day-vision began to fade

> *at that moment my friends stumbled onto*
> *the amphitheater and we all laughed*
> *at this incredible find*

> *when i told them of my day-vision*
> *they agreed the story brought an electricity*
> *to their inner selves*

> *i think many of us have had experiences*
> *where we feel a kind of energy coming at us*
> *this was that kind of feeling*

we soon made our way back to the vw beetle
as we drove down the mountain
the shadows of the sun were increasing
against the pine forest trees
i remember this vision well
and often visit it in my memory.

The Veins of My Soul

It runs through the veins of my soul that all religions are beautiful in their way:

The way we form a community, help each other survive and be safe and secure, and have meaning to our lives . . . and the way religion and community serve each other when they agree to approach God the same way.

But as I see it, the attitudes of these same communities can also be a cruel congregation of people when their belief is that they have the one and only true way to God. This is the tragedy of our religions, communities, and churches. And this is not beautiful at all to me.

It runs through the veins of my soul to ask:

Can we not agree on boundaries where no one has a right to harm, oppress, deceive, dominate, interfere with, or demean another's belief in God?

Can we not agree on boundaries of war, where war is only fought when the leaders are themselves willing to be on the front lines of the war zone, and where their spouses and their children also must serve?

Can we not agree to see the earth as a gift from God that we are expected to care for, where our prosperity does not give permission to forsake it?

Can we do this because it is our gift to future generations — to leave them an earth better than the one we have in order to live on forever?

Though these thoughts run through the veins of my soul, I am unfortunately unsure how to pass them on to others to make a difference.

Turkey Creek Contact

At Turkey Creek contact was made
the creek full of sounds
that rolled over rocks in the shallows and deep pockets

the willows and the tall grass bent
in the mild autumn breeze
the birds above the water soared low
between the canyon walls
the squirrels scampered up the trees
all kinds of insects doing their part in the dance

Then suddenly there were the wild boars
staring us down with warning eyes

And so it was that we shared the trail
the birds and the boars and the other creatures unseen

We sat under a group of willows
to take in the coolness of the creek

Refreshed and eyes closed at Turkey Creek
contact was made
and every living thing around us
made contact as well

> *there was evidence that God had been there*
> *you could see it*
> *feel it*
> *and sense it*
> *in the air*
> *— God was there*

in the creek
in the willows
in the wildflowers
in the grass
and on the trail

in every track made by every creature
the signs of God's presence were clear

at turkey creek contact was made
connecting all of us with God that day.

The Animals

most likely — the animals worship God
in a way we cannot understand

most likely — we worship God
in a way the animals cannot understand.

The Rabbit Was Still

the rabbit was still
the morning cold
not a breeze astir

across the meadow
two foxes chased a rabbit
still and silent

ever so gradually and sure
the sun peeked
over the distant hill

if this were the last day
for the earth
or the first for us

i do not think the rabbits
the foxes
the breeze
or the sun
would have given it
much thought

> *so where do the rabbits*
> *foxes*
> *wind*
> *and sun*
> *fit into God's plan?*

Does Our Spirit Flow

After nearly two hours the musician finishes the last piece of music, then rises from the chair. She is caught up in an ecstasy of the music she has just performed, and her testimony is that the sensation flowing through her to her hands is her spirit.

It is a mystery how she can be so sure this is the feeling of her spirit flowing—is it flowing through her hands or some kind of emotional high she only imagines as a spiritual force?

An artist I know speaks of the same kind of sensation that courses through his hands and onto the canvas, and I have read about a missionary in a remote region of the world who seems to feel the same way as he distributes food and reaches out to those in need. The missionary says that at times it seems a touch of his hand is a reassuring gesture that goes far beyond the physical touch itself.

Does our spirit indeed flow through us in these ways?

I've heard doctors and nurses discuss this phenomenon, for there are many occasions when patients want the touch of a hand to soothe their fear and pain.

I've witnessed how the touch of a parent soothes a child and how the animal responds to the kind touch of the human.

I accept all these testimonies as real.

Evidence Versus Sign

he said:

*the day started good
and ended badly
and i was puzzled by it*

*because i see it as a sign
that if the day starts out good
it means the whole day
is supposed to be good*

*and if the day starts badly
i see it as a sign
that the whole day
is supposed to be bad*

*and if the day turns out differently
from its start
then it has no effect on my belief that —*

> *how the day starts
> is supposed to be
> how the day will progress
> and end*

i asked myself:

*why is it that if certain evidence
of a belief contradicts that belief
we are still not convinced that our belief
may not be as true as we suppose?*

Facing Death

the idea of facing death
before experiencing
the life i want to live
haunts me
gives me no peace
causes me anxiety
even to think
about it

if i could live
enough of the life i wanted
and be somewhat satisfied
then death would have
no sting for me —
absolutely

it is not the unanswered questions
that lie beyond death's door
that haunt me
but rather not having
the time or means or circumstances
to live the life i want.

The Seed Is the Greatest

the seed is one of the greatest creations of all
something so small that produces a harvest
upon which we thrive

if we learn how to plant and care for the seed
then our harvest is ensured
is this not then true for all seeds?

   – seeds of compassion and tolerance
   – seeds of hate and intolerance

just name it
if we nurture it
it will grow.

my theology is

there is no way to go but up
    — when we die

we all go to heaven for there is no hell
    — only mercy

our flaws are not our problem
    — they are the Creator's
and the Creator does not burden us
    — with a problem only He can solve

there are no beliefs in God that excel over others
    — there are only opinions and speculations

we judge our own behavior on the earth
    — and rightly so
but concerning our life beyond the earth
    — we are not judges of anyone's destiny

there are judgments that are God's
and judgments that are ours
    — let us be not eager to take on what is not ours
equality of and consideration and respect for all humans
    — should be a given

our spirit untouched by sin
and perfect in every way
    — makes it predetermined that our spirit goes to
    heaven

bodies and minds and hearts
the imperfect parts
they choose either good or evil

therefore they will die and cease
    — to exist

it is an unsure journey
as we are burdened with faith
in an unseen and silent God
    — mostly

let us give each other some room
    — on this planet

let us learn to treat others as we want
to be treated
    — and live longer.

Infinite Universe

infinite universe
how shall i confirm
my existence
and give meaning
to life?

is it my discovery
of You that will
provide this
meaning
and an expectation
for tomorrow?

Is Mercy Your Plan

mercy of God
Your silence to us
is unnerving

we want
a sign from You
of love

we wait all the day long
till night comes to us

mercy of God
what does Your si-
lence mean?

if You reprimand us not
then are You satisfied
with your creation?

and if not
is mercy
Your plan?

I Can Love a Merciful God

creatures in need of mercy
i imagine Your mercy extended to us
    — the only way to bury our flaws

You are the only power with this mercy over our lives
as it is Your flaw as well
for we are Your creation and Your mercy will relieve You
    — of our created flaws

so whether extended mercy grows from a need
beyond our understanding
and whether extended mercy grows from a love
for us and our burden
it matters little
    — as long as it is mercy

i believe in the "all merciful God"
i am bound to God
controlled by God
and God asks nothing of me to prove my love
for it seems as if the burden of proof is in God's hand

> *You control all*
> *have made all*
> *decide the fate of all*
>
> *and need not Your "created"*
> *to prove to You its love*
>
> *i can love a merciful God*
> *who takes upon Himself*
> *the burden of His creation.*

God Is Alive and Well

> God is alive and well
> it is only we who are not

We are ill with theology and doctrine, gluttoned by the dreams of heaven and hell.

The thoughts of reward and punishment haunt us, though we admit it not.

> God is alive and well
> and God's mercy
> waits for us at our end

For it is we who have created a mercy full of punishment and hell.

Thank God that God's mercy has not the vocabulary for punishment or hell.

Can we not believe in a God of mercy like this?

> God is alive and well
> and God has a place in our soul

Be still and learn of the God that resides in us; seek God within, where God is found.

May we seek not to impose upon God our own guilt

> — as if He too considers us guilty.

I Felt Like a Baptist Today

I had been spending time at home, so much so that when my wife and I went to a music festival in the park I soon noticed my intolerance of anything and everyone who was not conforming to my view of life. I chuckled and snubbed the people in the park as they passed by, so much so that I felt like a Baptist—safe in my conviction.

No, I will not become as the Baptist, firm on my own pedestal of righteousness.

Yes, I will enjoy the music and the afternoon at the park, and let everyone else do the same.

I Have Not Seen God

i have not seen God
but i believe God has seen me

i do not think we are friends yet
though i believe i have spoken to Him

most likely this relationship
will be one where i do all the talking

where God controls the nature
of the relationship and how it will progress

i guess that is the way it is
in relationships between Gods and humans

i do hope we can be friends
but i fear i have nothing to give
to the friendship that God needs.

Is It Up to Us

Is it up to us to rule or be ruled?
Why do we insist that God takes sides?

If it is up to us to rule and if God allows us to rule
or be ruled without any intervention on his behalf
then in reality it could be that God is not on any side.

Why are we not convinced of this?

And why is it in our nature to insist that God take sides
and intervene on our behalf in the matters we choose?

The Truth about Truth

The truths that we believe we know about God are wrapped in our imagination—and we must believe our imagined truth about God through faith, which requires no proof other than our passion to believe and defend it.

I believe that we believe the mystery of our faith reaches to the heavens where God dwells and where it becomes truth.

I believe we have great confusion in discerning faith from imagination, for these are just words that attempt to describe the truths we all seek.

Perhaps some new words are required to move us along this path better.

How is that for truth?

Hiking in the Gila

1.
hiking offers exercise and therapy and renewal
new experiences for mind and body and heart and spirit
hiking is a soulful endeavor
where the effort builds character

— without fail.

2.
both scenery and hiking ministers to my soul

it is a sermon i have never heard or sensed
until that moment in time

hiking is being ministered to

— if i am willing.

3.
after a hike i feel small
because i can see i will not ever
be equal in stature
to a forest

— i am the student.

Cat and Mouse

the cat saw the mouse
        and could not look away
as though it were
        the cat's moral obligation
to trap and eat the mouse

the other mice watching
        had no moral obligation
sensed no need to retaliate
        nor had the desire
to turn the other cheek

hence evidence of the difference
        between animals and humans.

Mercy of God

mercy of God
extend Your hand
to Your creation
—we are Your flaw

mercy of God
judge us not for creating
theologies and messiahs
—in Your name

mercy of God
we thought we
could amend
— what You have made

mercy of God
blame us not
for any crime
—we have committed

mercy of God
take upon Yourself
the flaws of
—Your own creation

mercy of God
send us all
to the same place
—after we die

mercy of God
may i rest in peace
knowing You will make good
— by Your creation

mercy of God
take away the flaws
and sins of our life
and let the fault of them
— be upon You

mercy of God –
        my theology
        my creed
        my doctrine.

On Worship

i do not believe God needs

or requires our worship

but accepts it.

Notes for the Source

I see better when I slow myself down.

The fear of living a life I do not want requires a fast pace.

There is nothing I seek more in life than to know You.

> *— and while i am in the pursuit of You*

I want to be kind
I want to be contemplative not noisy
I want to wise in my contributions to conversation
I want to be nonjudgmental unless absolutely necessary
and then only sparingly
I want to have integrity and a quietness and a peace about me

I want to be known as an honest and true man
I want to be known as a considerate man
I want to be known as a man who takes care of his body
I want to lack for nothing in a fairly conservative and
frugal way
I want to be truly content with what I have and learn to
take care of what I have
I want to be indebted to none

I want to know what it is to be loved by a woman
and to know what it is to love the woman who loves me

> *— and while i am in the pursuit of You*

I am better when I can move slowly and discern the lives
around me

> *— that is why my prayer is that You show me how.*

One Day This Came

The seeking of God is a personal venture and the truth of it is mostly in spiritual terms.

It is a part of my life that gives me a peace in living and, hopefully, in dying.

I am learning to know my place in the world through seeking God in the spirit.

I believe the spirit realm is a reality different from the mind, body, and heart.

I believe the spirit has the power to change the mind, body and heart; therefore the spirit is a guide for my life.

In my search I have found my spirit and I have come to know of God through its finding.

The proof of my knowing God is in the value I place on the lives of others around me in everyday life. It seems God wants us to care for us, and that it is up to us.

> *i claim no religious affiliation*
> *i only pursue God in the way*
> *i am moved to do so.*

Private Matter

It is a private matter — the relationship between God and me.

It is by my deeds and actions towards people and the earth that my religious beliefs are lived, as evidenced in my life, which is more of a true testimony of what I believe than my words.

I think it will take a lifetime of practice before any of us can be judged by God, if ever.

Questions for Travelers

1.

if we are the travelers
you and i

and

the earth is only
a vessel

then

who is the captain?

if the rules of the vessel
are for us

to treat each other
with respect

then

what happens to us
if we do not abide?

if this earth vessel is ours
to steer or destroy

then

what is the reward or
punishment for success or failure?

2.
where are we going
will we eventually arrive at our destination
or is there no destination?

if we are travelers upon this earth vessel

and

if we have no real instructions

then

do you think we could at least
have the sense to look after one another and the vessel
while we make the journey?

do you think we could leave it in good shape
for the next travelers?

just a thought.

Frank K., 3:10 p.m., September 23

Frank K. conversed over coffee, his words inaudible some of the time. . . .

1.
how to set a horse
    — trust

how to be a successful executive
    — watch your back and look forward

how to keep up
    — listen

how to focus
    — peripheral vision.

2.
My remarks upon reading some other people's remarks concerning Frank K. . . .

    not everyone likes frank
    not everyone likes me
    not everyone likes you

so there

put it to rest.

3.

Another conversation with Frank K. at a later date. . . .

if a man i do not like is in need of emergency help

i will help

i know if i do not help

it will be a defeat of my character.

4.

i am lonely mostly because i believe i am superior

i do not voice it . . . but i think it for sure.

The Mornings Are Quiet

1.
the mornings are quiet here
and that being so
i reflect upon my life as a prayer
and look inward and outward as if at prayer

i imagine millions of people pray
in a similar or different manner
so which kind of prayer does God hear?
cannot we give each person as much right to God
as we give ourselves?

is not our own reach for God equal to all others?
why is it so important that our way of prayer
be superior to theirs?

2.
the mornings are quiet here
and that being so
i reflect upon my life as a prayer
and look inward and outward as if at prayer

i imagine that i go straight to the Source
while others may imagine that they must go
through a Messiah to reach It
i believe we can all reach the Source if we only reach out

and then there will always be those
who are angered by statements like this
which cause them to pray to the Source
in their judgment against people like me

i believe those prayers are a waste of time
that instead they should use that time of prayer
for guidance for their own lives
and leave the judgment of how God should treat others to
God.

3.
the mornings are quiet here
and that being so
i reflect upon my life as a prayer
and look inward and outward as if at prayer.

The Depths

the depths of my wants are more simple
the deeper i go into myself
for it is there where the simpler life is found
and the joy is easier achieved

if i stay at the shallow end
where the ease of reasoning is found
then my peace becomes wrapped up
in the cloak of worldly wants

not that i do not want these wants
or that the wants are wrong
but when i go deeper into myself
these wants become not my aim in life

> *the more i go to the shallow end*
> *the more these wants become*
> *too important.*

The Loss Was Too Great

The building burned, and with it also burned all the beautiful solid oak paneling and all the hardwood pews and the choir loft with the hanging wrought iron-cased lights and all the incredible stained glass windows. The large stained glass cross behind the pulpit burned as well. Four generations of tradition all incinerated that night.

The congregation could not afford to replicate the beauty of the church along with the two-story brick building and all the wrought-iron fencing and landscaping. The members wept loudly, as if God had forsaken them by allowing their sanctuary to burn and by making refugees of them. The loyalty of this congregation to their rites and their creed was undeniable. So how could their God allow this? What had they done to deserve this? How could they worship anywhere else or build another church like this one?

While this loss of faith was occurring, immense as it was, and the priest was struggling to reestablish his flock's faith, across the globe wars and oppression still raged in regions where this church had given much aid. The congregants reminded themselves that they had given much to those areas and contributed much to the humanitarian needs of those regions, and so began to ask themselves how God could not honor their contributions. These kinds of thoughts caused such grief that it was impossible to overcome. *They felt their loss was too great.*

They thought as long as they performed their duties and rites, God should have no grievance against them and should protect them against such tragedies. Yet they felt untroubled by the tragedies occurring every day all over the world — where there are no churches — nor homes, full stomachs, parents, or medicine. They thought as long as they "gave something" God would look after them in the way they had chosen to interpret.

These congregants did not allow themselves to see what it was they did have, nor let that truth heal them of the loss of their building. They could see no further than their own tragedy, and began to ask why they believed at all in a God that would allow such an act. *The loss was too great.*

And the saddest thing of all? That the four generations in the church and all the scripture read aloud every Sunday were insufficient to remedy their perceived victimization. They could not see how very secluded and protected their lives were from the real needs of the world. This congregation refused to see that they could be thankful for what they did have. The loss of their church building was too great for them to bear, and their consideration for any other suffering of any other people seemed a distant second to this concern. *Their loss was too great.*

Many never returned to that church, or any church, for they vowed it would and could never be the same. In their eyes God had forsaken them and they would not and could not ever forget. They could not and would not be consoled, for the building was their prize and their glory from God, their reason to give and help others.

. . . *Their loss was too great.*

To Cry for Our Own

to cry only for our own
to feel only our own loss
to see not the tears we bring to those we fight
is a selfish sorrow

though we feel pain for our loss
it may not cause us to care
for the loss we bring to our enemies

> *until we feel the loss*
> *the sorrow*
> *and the pain*
> *of those we fight*
> *we will never see peace*
> *any other way*
> *than through war*

and words like these
will remain hollow
to those who can weep only
for a loss of their own.

The Narrow Gate

The man proclaimed, "Enter through the narrow gate."

But I was unable to see the virtue of such a narrow gate, at least in the way he described it, for the man on the stage was as narrow in mind, as full of judgment, and as intolerant as he described the gate to be — though I believe he was unable to see himself as I have depicted him.

I think maybe he had entered the wrong narrow gate, if it was to be the narrow gate that would lead us to God.

I think he would not like my speaking of him like this either. On the other hand, he is the one at the pulpit making the claims.

The Most Honest of Faiths

The most honest of faiths in God is one that would include us all. Every style of worship and every attempt to reach out to Him would be considered beautiful.

I go, therefore, in faith, knowing I will not be turned away. The worship of God is a realm all its own; there are no guarantees other than that.

> *though i am unhealed*
> *and i receive no protection from God*
> *i am always welcome*
>
> *though i plead with God*
> *i may not ever receive*
>
> *yet i can go and worship*
> *and be filled spiritually*
> *almost anytime*

I ask, what is it that God will give?

From this place of worship I see only my spirit reaching for God. Though my soul is lifted to a special place that is all I receive.

In my own loneliness I see the loneliness of others and I learn to care
My worship has taken me to the place where I am learning to care.

> *i see this as the most honest of faiths.*

1967 in a Small Town in New Mexico

When we were kids, about 11, 12, or 13, we occasionally took our 22s or 20-gauge shotguns out into the woods, which were about half a mile or so from our houses.

The narrow paved road led away from the few homes and into the open meadows and low rolling hills.

The way I remember it, as we made our sojourn an occasional police officer would spot us and lecture us about walking in the middle of the road — it was stupid, he'd say, we could get run over, and this was not something our parents would appreciate.

I guess back then for a group of boys to meander down the road with guns was no threat or danger, whereas walking in the middle of the road was paramount as it meant we might be disobeying our parents.

It Is Us

He was sure it was God speaking to him because it agreed with him.

Although the task he believed God gave him was difficult and unusual, it still agreed with him.

To this man the tasks of this nature seemed to prove God all the more, no matter how outrageous and irrational the task might be.

Why did this man need to impose this nature upon God and then sell it to others as a spiritual understanding?

Why is it that the spiritual has to be irrational, unusual, outrageous, and difficult in order to prove it is God, and why are we compelled to think up concepts like this to prove God is?

This is what the man said the voice of God told him:

"go to the mountain and fast three days
and wait for Me to speak

I will show you then what it is you are
to do when you return

wear a red hat into the church
those who say nothing are of Me
and those who comment on it are not of Me

remember it is I who will touch
each person to respond as he does."

The man did as he was told, sure after he did that he knew now who was of God and who was not of God in this church.

And so it is that we live in this kind of world and make decisions in this way, believing God speaks in this manner.

But why would God make such absurd requests and work in such secretive and mysterious ways?

I think it is mostly that we and our own self-created mythology cast God in such a role as this.

The No-help God

the no-help-from-God realization
does not make God questionable
but it makes God real to see God
as not offering "intervention" help
most of the time

If we can only believe in God if He is involved in our lives with miracles, healings, and interventions, then we either become numb to the failure of God's performing for us in that way or we lose our concept of God completely.

Instead of always seeking miracles and healings and interventions, I believe we must learn to seek guidance and then learn to take the steps ourselves.

step back and take a good look
learn of this God that created us
and controls us in this way

i believe that anyone who seeks God for guidance
will learn of God this way
and not be disappointed

perhaps this "no-intervention/help" God
is the truer picture
if so it is an important truth to see
as our future may very well depend upon it.

The Story Seemed Absurd

His story was absurd. The man said that God had told him to stand outside the shopping mall and proclaim the message of salvation to the people as they passed by, to not hesitate to speak out the words that God had given him, "to speak and leave nothing out."

The man said, "Your God, the devil, keeps you from the true God, but if you repent and confess Jesus as Lord and as the Son of God then God will show you mercy, and after you leave earth you will spend eternity with Him. If you do not do this then you will spend eternity in Hell."

To the man, this statement made perfect sense, as he believed the power of these words would cause all humans to come to God and be saved. Therefore the man believed no further reason had to be given for why he spoke and why he believed he was accountable to no man for what he did or said; rather, he believed he was only accountable to the God he served.

The Way Home

how do i find my way home
after diverging from the path i know
onto paths that seemed right at the time?

    is it knowing where to look and how to look that is the key?

alone for a time i seek the quiet places in my soul
and then rise from the quietness and join the others

    is it there i test the new strength i found
    in my search for the way home?

i go there often now and return again to the world
to test my finds among others
then retreat again
then rise again to face the world

so it is in the quietness of my soul i go
and listen and search until the path
opens to me the way home

and when i stray i retreat
to find myself again
and again.

This Kind of Evolution

We started out with an idea of how things would be and from there the idea evolved.

As we tried to live the idea it evolved more through the process of living it.

So what we have now is different from the original idea, although as I look back it is probably no better than the original.

It seems every idea evolves, some for the better and some for the worse; some live on and some die, but nonetheless continue to evolve.

I believe our beliefs in God evolve over time and change to where the original is not the same as it was at inception.

What we believe in today will more than likely evolve into a different belief with the passing of time.

When it comes to these spiritual ideas of God, they will evolve and we will believe these ideas as if they have not evolved.

Somehow we have it in our heads that evolution of any kind is wrong, so we fight this idea that our spiritual beliefs are transformative.

But who's to say? Perhaps God does evolve.

Certainly the universe provides the evidence that all existence evolves, including the planet.

This Thought

this thought is full of holes
yet could float as well any other thought

this thought can be compared to most
spiritual doctrinal views
for they are also full of holes
and yet seem to have floated for centuries

i watch a very large woman struggle to stand up from her
chair at a café
she moves very slowly to the counter as if in slow motion

the growing weight problem in our country is alarming
like a sadness manifested through us

i do not know anyone who wants to be as large as this
woman
perhaps the survival of the fittest is the only real way to
solve the obesity problem.

Open Country

my soul is like an open country
where the land is for the taking
where i can build where and what i want
fence it in or let it remain untouched

my soul was given to me
to do with as i want.

Two Poems for Chip

1. *Chip says to his daughter*

I'm not going to let it get me down 'cause I have you.

There are pretty flowers in the field, red and yellow and purple and orange.

There is a sky that flies above, blue and white, and clouds that are bright.

There is a sun that takes the day from light to dark and dark to light.

I'm not going to let it get me down 'cause I have you.

As long as there is life in me and life in you, it is life enough for me to love.

It is your smile and it is your laughter, your kisses, and your hugs that keep me smiling all the day long.

I'm not going to let it get me down 'cause I have you.

2. *Every day*

every day i will walk
    because i can

i have legs and i have arms
i have ears and i have eyes
i have a mind and i have a heart
i am of body and i am of spirit

i am free to walk if i want
so every day i will walk
    because i can.

when my breath fails
when my life changes
maybe then will i see it differently
but today my life calls me to it

so every day i will walk
    because i can.

My Musician

The beauty of your music is that you carry it with grace and excitement.

The movement of your fingers follows your spirit as it moves with a rhythm that lives in you.

It is more than a melody that you share; the music comes from the inside.

You are my musician, for you take me where I cannot go and you give me what I do not have.

I am with you — as you bring forth the music that is in you.

there is worship in your music and you go there often
to play for your God who is the Source of it all

make the most of the time
and may the joy of it all be there for you in the moment
may it fill your soul completely and overflow onto us

let the serenade begin.

A Wedding Place for My Niece

1.

In looking for a wedding place for my niece we remembered the monastery, so off we went.

In the mountains of the Gila National Forest there lies a most beautiful Catholic monastery. The scenery and the architecture of the building seem to merge into one identity, in this place where man attempts a relationship with nature and God.

The sanctuary is saddled on the top of a mountain crest where the view goes on farther than the eye can see. The brothers and the priests of this monastery walk in a harmony all their own and are willing to share it with any who are willing to listen — and with great zeal.

2.

As I listened to one brother share the gospel according to the Catholic monks, he also added his message, that this monastery was built and paid for by the Catholic Church, and was for Catholics only. Obviously I had to become a Catholic if I were to have access to it and enjoy it.

I was inquiring about a location for the wedding of my niece, who had no religious affiliation. Was not this beautiful monastery in the mountains an ideal place for wedding vows?

I assumed these monks would be enthused to assist in the event, and was jolted to find out how wrong I was. I had to accept the fact that this monastery and all its settings were For Catholics Only. It seemed the monks and the priests here had lost the knowledge that there were believers who could exist and find approval from God outside the Catholic Church.

3.

I replied by pointing out to the young monk that Christ had never told His "message" this way, but the monk could not see it. Though he did say Christ was for everyone, which actually meant that the Catholic theology was for everyone and that no other theology was approved of by God.

Which made it easy to say that this monastery was For Catholics Only.

I conceded. I had to accept his words on the grounds that the Catholic Church was financing the monastery and therefore it was theirs to do with as they wished.

But the strangest part of this conversation was that the monk could not accept my surprise at his comments, and reiterated again that my niece and I were simply not welcome unless we converted to Catholicism.

Clearly, "honesty and truth" of this sort do not immediately bring us closer to God, though they might in time if only we could realize the blindness of this kind of faith.

I tried to take no offense for this man's truth, but truth is how truth is . . . and the truth is that only Catholics will be married in this monastery.

Missing God

we seem to be missing God
it seems God is willing to be missed

we create theologies bibles doctrines
denominations and religions
all in the name of God

i think all that matters
is that we learn how to care for one another
and be less intolerant about how each of us
might view our relationship
to this God.

It Goes On and On and On and On

If God is only known in the spiritual realm, and we are
the ones dissatisfied and trying to force things into the
emotional, mental, and physical realms, then perhaps the
effort we put forth in wanting the emotions, the mind, and
the body to be as the spirit is the failure of our faith.

Let us go into the spiritual place to worship; let us pray
and seek to commune with God and bring back an
understanding about how we can live in this more total
realm . . .

> *where our emotions and mind and body*
> *are in better harmony with the spirit*
> *and where faith is the connection to harmony*

It goes on and on and on, our quest for God, as if each of
us has to come to terms with a God.

For me the quest is seeking in my spirit a place where
harmony dwells and where faith guides me there.

> *— and it is there I will look for God.*

Giving Our Word

1.

at twelve years old
a friend gave me his word
and i took it seriously

i wanted his word to be good
when it was not i was upset

now at age fifty-four
when friends give me their word
i still take it seriously

if their word turns out to be not good
i still get upset about it

> *although i expect it to happen every now and then*
> *because i have seen it happen with my word as well*

when we give people our word
we should take it seriously
and guard it well.

2.

when i have put forth untruthful words
and then stood by them
that is a sting that remains with me

when i have put forth truthful words
and have not stood by them
that is also a sting that remains with me

the lesson is learning how to give some slack
on this mighty issue of *giving one's word*.

Walk the Plank

In his dream, a young man with colon cancer saw himself at the edge of a ship, tied and blindfolded, and then ordered to jump into the ocean.

He said: "There on the edge I said to myself, *I will walk the plank and jump into the ocean and fight to swim, till at last I give up.*

"I have seen my future and it is a haunting revelation to be so caught up in the spirit, and know God watches and does nothing."

What a mystery — to see our own future and experience a power beyond that could so graciously heal the cancer, but instead does nothing about it, only offering us a dream of our own death.

This dream shared leaves me no peace.

My question is: If God has the ability to make the difference, why doesn't He?

When the Fire of Love Is Wrong

If we are the kindling, where is the match that will light the fire?

If our hands were to touch the fire, would it be too late to stop it?

If a gust of wind suddenly caused us to touch the flame, would the fire be fanned for sure?

If so, would we burn for hours till our desire was filled?

How did it happen, that it has become this way for you and me?

may the match never be lit
may the breeze not stir
we do not love as love should love
nor do we know how to manifest such a love

all we do is start the fires as if love were a flame
one moment is all it takes to be engulfed
with a love that has no boundary or foundation
can we not learn to make a better love that endures?

be persuaded my readers not to dream for so long that it
blinds you from reality
if our dreams could remain dreams and still satisfy such
desires
millions of souls would bow at our feet to learn how to
dream such fantasies and be filled without the need to live
them out

When is the fire of love right? I say when there is enough warmth and light to last beyond one night.

When is the fire of love right? I say, when it satisfies us so we can sleep till the dawn and awaken rested.

When is the fire of love right? I say, when the excitement of it is so full of life that it makes all the days after right.

Men and the Rain

Two Christian neighbors, one replacing a roof, the other planting a garden, were waiting to see if the rain would come. The first needed clear skies to affix the roof; the other rain to water his seeds.

Each prayed for his own desire and, seeing himself as a good and righteous man, assumed that God would surely answer his prayer.

So when the men heard each other's prayer a chill ran through their bones. The dilemma was clear: How would God choose which man to bless?

> *. . . as if the deciding factor for God would be which man was "better"*
> *. . . as if God were in indecision as to which prayer to answer*
> *. . . as if the rain were controlled by the prayers of people*

The rain, when it came, watered the garden and also did great harm to the unfinished roof, but each man had no choice but to accept the offering for what it was and appraise the event as neither a blessing nor a non-blessing from God.

This event did not make the men better friends, only more suspicious and cautious of each other.

Under a Spell

we are under a spell
taken in by what we want
to be true

when we are intolerant of all other beliefs
it is obvious we are under a spell

for the goal of the spell
is to divide us and separate us
and cause us to justify prejudice and cruelty
toward anyone who disagrees
with what we "know" to be true.

Rockslides

perhaps

the rocks of our beliefs
have turned into rockslides
where we care not that we tumble them
upon those who do not believe as we do

i see

these rockslides
as the belief that we have a better belief than the rest
that it is our mission from God to convert all to that belief
and to be intolerant of any other belief in God

this is a rockslide for sure.

What If

1.

Has God inspired man to write His Word to us? If so, which one is the right one?

What if God writes in the spirit only and we must search there to find it—how will we know it when we do?

Will we know because what is written in our spirit will be the same for us all?

2.

If we realize that none of us wants to be cheated, oppressed, treated cruelly, or lied to by anyone else, and that we prefer others to treat us as we want to be treated, then it could be that God wants us to behave in this way.

Could this be one example of God's writing His word in our spirit?

what if . . . ?

Thirty Sayings . . . More Or Less

It should be obvious

We may think we know a few things about God, but all we think we know for sure is uncertain. My best guess is that only God knows God (a concept based on the C.S. Lewis poem, "Footnote to All Prayers").

The yarn

The yarn is that we know for sure of the existence of heaven and hell — and that we know how to tell who is going there.

Arrogance

The irony of arrogance is its insistence on being right all the time.

The problem with capitalism

The problem with capitalism is that it wants the freedom to care about what it wants to care about, and it may not be you. For the average citizen that is a problem.

Expectant believer

If I have not sinned all week, am I entitled to one this week? Is that how it works?

A great thing

I dreamed I converted a Buddhist to Christianity — as if it were a good thing.

Paths

There are many paths to God. The point of it all is to become a better human being while on the earth.

Fear not knowledge

Fear not knowledge; rather fear what we do with the knowledge.

Fear to think

The fear to think wrongly about a thing we do not understand is a superstition of the most dangerous kind.

Forgive and forget

Either be willing to be held accountable for everything you do and say — or have good friends who are willing to forgive and forget.

On gifts and virtue

A talented person may not necessarily live a virtuous life. We must not turn these gifts and talents away because of this contradiction. Virtue may not necessarily produce a gifted or talented person. We must not keep insisting it does.

An American patriot's view of liberation

We invade, then we cause chaos, then we abandon. To us this is a liberating experience.

I heard a saying that went like this

Behave how you want to be remembered.

Keep the earth flat

If our view of the gods cannot be challenged, then the goal of the gods is to keep the earth flat and to rule by fear . . . and to keep us from straying too far.

Knock knock, who's there?

Do we knock at the world's door or does the world knock at our door?

Meaning of life

Could it be that the more we value life the more possible it is to know its meaning?

Laughter

Laughter can be blindness to the fool and healing for the wise.

Good-sounding words

If we lie not, steal not, and sleep well, we will wake with better health and a clear mind and a keen eye. But what if this does not work? Words that sound good may not always contain the most reliable truth.

Lies and truth

1.
One lie leads to another, until at last it changes you.

2.
Truth is our start in life. We should keep it as close to us as we can, so when we leave the earth we will hopefully have enough left to send us on our way.

3.
Though truth is free, it has a cost.

4.
In time a lie could cost everything that is important in life, so be careful what you are willing to lie about.

5.
Truth is like a light that shows us the path home. Though the path may be rough it is truth that will light the way, and it is we who must make the effort to take the steps to see where that light leads.

Not his favorite

It is not possible that we are the best of God's creation; more likely we are not His favorite one either.

Innocence and a problem

There is none innocent; that is why we act the way we do. The problem is God has a problem and we are it. So whose responsibility is it to solve?

Power

Does power corrupt or does power attract the corrupt, or both?

Opinions and friends

If we could treat friends as our opinions and hold on to them whether they are right or wrong, that might be good. If we could treat opinions as friends and let them go when they don't fit us, that might be good. Then we might know which is more important.

Rainbows

I have chased rainbows for so long that I have forgotten my way home.

How to be alone

I have forgotten how to forgive, and now I am alone all the time.

Humans and animals

Why do animals act human and humans act like animals? Though we are not like the other animals, we are no less animal.

The animals

Most likely the animals worship God in a way we cannot comprehend, and we worship God in a way they cannot comprehend either.

How to communicate with the birds and other animals

The way to communicate with the birds and the other
animals is to learn their language or to teach them ours.
If you don't believe me then you try talking to the birds
without knowing their language and see where that will
get you.

To believe we know God

To believe we know God is to make Him less God . . .
To believe we know God is to make us more God . . .
To believe we know God is a start in the wrong direction.

On patience, paths, and pain

Is it that patience is mostly learned through experience?
The path to a livable happiness is not necessarily
accomplished by figuring out God . . .
The pain we feel that is caused by our selfishness destroys
us . . . in time.
The pain we feel that is caused by our compassion builds
us . . . in time.

To spill

If our lives must spill over onto others around us, then I
would rather spill something good than bad.

What I know about love

Please believe me when I say I hardly know a thing about
love. I would believe you if you were the one to have said
it.

What is wrong with these statements

Without war we have no need of soldiers . . .
Without greed we have no need of servants . . .
Without sin we have no need of Saviors.

True value

The true value of our belief is based upon the value we
place on other people, and it is probably a good idea to
include all the living on the earth.

What we need

What we need are laws to protect us from each other or a
heart of gold so we don't want to harm anyone else.

Wisdom of hindsight

My prayer to God this night is to grant me the wisdom of
hindsight today for tomorrow — and the ability to do no
harm.

My faith

My faith is personal and I would do well to keep it that
way, for the moment I proclaim my faith as the answer for
another is the moment my faith begins to fail.

Consider These

1.
when my spirit worships You
my mind and heart and body follow
there is no doctrine or theology or tithe or church or song
that can instruct me better
for they are only instruments of mine to use as i want
i am not their slave and God never intended me to be.

2.
in a single act of kindness the need for doctrine
and theology and tithe and church begins to fade.

Why Would God Be Willing

I know a young girl of eight years old who suffers from a neurological disorder and is slowly losing all use of her body.

Until she is healed why would God be willing to care so much about our lesser problems?

You and I must go to the back of the "God intervention" line, for there are others who have greater need.

Dance Spirit Dance

1.

i say to my spirit
dance spirit dance
along the ridge line
where the clouds
meet the mountains

i will find You there
i will take what You offer
and not pine for what
You offer not

though i may find You
on the mountain
no freedom am i guaranteed
even though i have climbed the distance

what does my spirit seek in You?
what is it You offer
and what is it You offer not?

2.

As I make my way down the mountain I so much want to bring God with me, but all I am allowed to bring back is what God has offered me there. And though I am empty of miracles and healings and intervention I still seek them, and I must be honest here and confess that it seems God does not promise or supply these upon request or even upon need.

But the offerings of a spiritual experience for its momentary sense and memories are real and what God offers for the taking for any who goes to the mountain. So, as I descend, I bring with me a joy of the memory of my experience and a sense that a part of God is with me and willing to offer me guidance through the message of the value of treating others as we want to be treated.

3.
i say to my spirit
dance spirit dance
along the ridge line
where the clouds
meet the mountains.

The Passing of a Friend
(With fond memories I write this about my favorite art teacher and good friend)

dorothy dorothy dorothy my soul delights in your life

you gave us so much
and asked for so little

and you accomplished this by
living your life how you wanted

thank you

you were gentle and you were sure
you cared and you remembered

you were the kind of friend
we can only dream of being

thank you

p.s. i will see you later and perhaps often.

To Be One with the Great Spirit

the drum beat loud
and then soft

the chant was the same

the rhythm
of feet moved
in tune with
the drum

the great spirit
was invited to join in

    and that was all that mattered
    – to be one with the great spirit.

Voice

whose voice do i hear
mine or God's?

I walked out into the open air and stood at the edge of a mountain. There was no one there, though I thought I heard a voice.

But it was I; I was the voice speaking to myself about a plan I thought would solve a certain dilemma in which I found myself.

I wanted it to be God speaking to me, but as I stood on the mountain crest where I was camped I could see the distant mountains and the mountains beyond until they disappeared into the air.

And as I looked toward the mountains I also looked inward and saw that the God I could see within me was not speaking.

But God has given me a spirit, which does speak to me, and my spirit is the voice I hear.

My question is: *Has God made us with enough within to live without the need of His voice speaking to us at every moment?*

I saw that day on that mountain that we have the needed spiritual knowledge to draw upon for the decisions we face in life.

And though the voice I heard was my own, it was drawing from a well of knowledge within me that had been given to me by God.

The Truth about Us

To unlock the truth about us may not be as important as learning how not to destroy ourselves and the earth.

For the fear of what we fear in each other can cause an evil in us to rise and not be satisfied until we have sought to rule over those we fear.

It seems the only true theology is that God allows us to do with the earth and ourselves as we please, and as to what happens after that, it is a mystery that we may never know.

if this is so then the important truth about us to learn
is how to unlock the ability
to learn how not to destroy ourselves and the earth.

Jesus, the Human

I bowed to my knees and then lay prostrate with my face on the ground. There I lifted up the name of Jesus so high I could not see him anymore.

It was not until I rose to my feet and could look Jesus in the eyes that I could see the real Jesus — the human.

I think the real Jesus was a human who was willing to stand for what he believed, who spoke out where he saw real injustice to others by the religious leaders of the day.

Jesus was a human willing to die for what he believed, and not bend. The miracle of it is that his message lives on and has changed the world.

I think the better truth is that Jesus was born human, died human, and spoke as a human with a message for humans.

> *to make Jesus more than human*
> *destroys the real Jesus*
> *the real miracle*
> *the real hope*
> *the real message*
> *is to treat others as you want them to treat you.*

The Greater Our God

The greater our God
the less inclined we
are to need God
to inflict punishment

In other words

the greater our God
the greater our belief
in the mercy of God

and our willingness
for all people to receive
this mercy is equal to
our belief in all beliefs
being equal in the
eyes of God.

I Will Care

i will care for the earth i have
seek peace with the neighbors i have
help those i can along my journey in life

Whether or not I come to know God and the ways of God,
I can know where it is I live, and who my neighbor is, and
who is in need of my help, and that is a more reliable peace
and a more sure meaning for my life than living to convert
others to a belief that I cannot know for sure is truth.

so i will care for the earth i have
seek peace with the neighbors i have
and help those i can along my journey in life.

I Bask

i bask in the late afternoon sun
while the shadows are moving in
gradual and quick the cold arrives
bursts and gusts
in the late afternoon breeze

february in southwest new mexico
the hills are beginning to turn
from greens and deep blues
into oranges yellows and purples

a storm is coming
perhaps it will be here
for the cool air is moist
and will turn the breeze into a wind
by sunup tomorrow

the sun the season the weather
this place allows me the time
to get away from other concerns.

Spirit Lessons

do we discover
our spirit
— is it there we
can go for
guidance?

is the evidence
of our being
guided by
the spirit
that we
consider
all people
as equal to
ourselves?

Works, Faith, and Mercy

1.

is it by faith or by works that we enter heaven?
i say neither
— that it is by mercy.

2.

so why have faith or works?
perhaps gratitude is enough of a reason.

3.

if we all receive the same mercy
because we all have the same need
then i will practice works
and faith out of gratitude
knowing God has granted me mercy
without condition of belief.

Is It in My Head

1.

my soul is home to my heart and mind and spirit
and my body possesses them all.

2.

my mind does think
my heart does feel
and my spirit does have faith.

3.

there is one God
and many paths to the same truth.

4.

are there as many paths
as there are people
and is God big enough
to minister to them all?

5.

i go not a day
without prayer
and pray without
noticing i pray.

6.

it is in me to seek
God for possible answers

and i think i will always
seek God for answers
and never give up
the seeking.

If Thou Allow

1.
if Thou allow O Lord
for us to do as we want
and if You do not
speak to us in words
where all people can agree

then do you speak at all
and are we left here to do as we please?

is our fate already sealed?

2.
if Thou, O Lord
be a merciful God
then are we to be
happy here on this earth?

if Thou O Lord
allow us a short
life till we die
and then are forgotten

then do we live happily on earth
with what short life we have?

3.
if Thou O Lord
are pleased with Thyself concerning us
then is it enough for me to have joy?

am i not to be concerned over the fate of my life?

if You do not make these truths known to me
am i guilty of living my life
without knowing for sure what You plan?

if there is no guilt then why do i feel shame?

is it in my shame that i know my life
is not altogether right
and so call out to You O Lord
is it enought to call out?

for to call out is a realization
of my need of a God to make my life right

so is Your silence as my friend
and is Your silence the message of Your mercy?

Ridgeline

1.
to climb the ridgeline
is to balance the way of
my normal life and
my gifted life

At times I descend from the ridgeline into my normal life and then make my way back up to the ridgeline only to descend onto the other side, into my gifted life.

Regardless into which life I descend, however, I need the ridgeline for its view in order to see both approaches and to have a reprieve from both. That is why the ridgeline is so important.

If I dared not climb the ridgeline at all I fear I would live in despair, for I am unable to live the normal or the gifted life only; I must live in them both. That is why when I do climb back up to the ridgeline and see both sides of me, my vision gives me some relief . . . but also despair, despair that I linger not too long in either of these ways.

For me, it is better to climb to the ridgeline to see what I am and then face the truth. For if I had never climbed I might never have seen either one — the gifted or normal me.

2.

i walk the ridgeline
where i balance between
the normal life and the gifted life
it seems each part of me has its own life
and its own truth

I must live both the gifted and the normal life to balance my sanity. If I descend into my gifted life and stay too long I might not climb back up, or I might forget how to climb back up, or I might lack the self-will to climb back up.

If I descend into the normal life and stay too long, I might not climb back either, for the fear of the loss of the gifted life might be too great, and I would therefore stay in the normal life rather than face the fear of climbing back up to the ridgeline only to find that I had lost my path back to my gifted life.

So I walk the ridgeline and descend into both sides till I have had my fill, and then climb back.

So it is that this kind of peace is only achieved through striving for it.

Will of Mine

Will of mine, reach for the depths of my being; let me take of what God has given me.

Let me become the wisdom, the strength, the peace, the quietness, the compassion, and the courage that I may live a prosperous and peaceful life with purpose . . .

that I may seek in the name of God these depths within me so that I might know myself in this way, become familiar with my depths, know how to be of help to others, and help them have a life of their own as well.

> *spirit of mine*
> *wake my will*
> *so i can face the burdens of this life*
> *though i may see no miracles or healings*
> *i am content*
>
> *with medical cures and inventions*
> *and new ways of solving old problems*
> *discoveries and new ideas*
> *make a difference*
>
> *will of mine*
> *reach for the depths of my being*
> *so i may take what God has given.*

I Am Convinced

I am convinced there is a God, that God wants to do us no harm, and that God is silent on much.

I am convinced that God's mercy awaits us all, regardless of our circumstances, beliefs, or behavior.

I am convinced that to be compassionate toward others and to look after the earth is our best answer while we are on the earth.

Character Versus Worship

if i confess You to others
in words and rituals and worship
then that is my witness of You

if i confess You to others
in character and conscience and behavior
then that is my witness of You

and the witness of my words
and ritual and worship cannot
ever equal the value of my
character conscience and behavior.

The Proof of All Beliefs

the proof of all beliefs is
not found in names
or buildings
or rituals

but in one's life.

In the End

if in the end i say i am acceptable to God
    and you say you are acceptable to God
then why are we fighting?

is it because we don't believe each other's testimony?

Concluding Notes

1.
we are of earth
and earth is
ours

we are of spirit
and our spirit is
God's.

2.
we are of body and mind and heart
and we stumble in body
and mind
and heart

our spirit is perfect
and our spirit
waits to go home.

3.
we are born to reach for God
and God waits for us to reach

we write books on pages
and God writes books in our spirit

so it is by our spirit
that we learn of God
and reach for God.

4.
we live forever
by the mercy of God
and we live forever in the spirit

our body and mind and heart cannot go
where our spirit goes.

5.
strive not to change anyone into our likeness
rather strive not to lie or cheat
or steal or deceive or use anyone
in a cruel or harmful way.

6.
could it be we are not guilty in an eternal court
even if we destroy another or destroy the earth
because our imperfect parts remain on the earth
and our perfect parts enter heaven
where the eternal court has not condemned us?

is "mercy for all" God's answer for our imperfect parts?

is it by mercy our spirit returns to its home?

we all seek a God
and i believe it is the same God

may we all find the answers we seek from our God
and may our God meet our need

and may we have a genuine peace
knowing the mercy of God patiently waits for us
till our last day.

About the Author

Tony Prewit was born in Stamford, Texas in 1954 and then moved with his family at the age of eight to Silver City, New Mexico. He has earned both bachelor's and master's of arts degrees and has traveled extensively throughout the United States as a musician. Besides his interest in poetry, the author has written, directed, and performed in several plays and as a mime actor. In addition, he is an artist who delves in photography, charcoals, pastels, and watercolors. Art is his private therapy.

For over thirty-five years the author kept a jounal of poetry that chronicled his most secret, inner struggles with his belief in God. During that time he lived what seemed to be a fairly normal life—traveling, going to school, marrying, and owning a retail furniture company. This journal, however, does not chronicle his "normal" life, but his struggles with belief. He believes many people have these same kinds of inner challenges with life, and this journal brings to the forefront the reality of these challenges.

Since 1978 he has lived with his wife Pat, a classical pianist, in Silver City, New Mexico, the place he considers home for its culture, land, seasons, and people.

www.ingramcontent.com/pod-product-compliance
Lightning Source LLC
Chambersburg PA
CBHW052115090426
42741CB00009B/1814